To VINNIE

Good Luck

STARTING AT THE FINISH LINE

Coach Al Buehler

STARTING AT THE FINISH LINE

COACH AL BUEHLER'S TIMELESS WISDOM

Amy E. Unell

with Barbara C. Unell and Bob Unell

A PERIGEE BOOK

A PERIGEE BOOK
Published by the Penguin Group
Penguin Group (USA) Inc.
375 Hudson Street, New York, New York 10014, USA

Penguin Group (Canada), 90 Eglinton Avenue East, Suite 700, Toronto, Ontario M4P 2Y3, Canada
(a division of Pearson Penguin Canada Inc.) • Penguin Books Ltd., 80 Strand, London WC2R 0RL,
England • Penguin Group Ireland, 25 St. Stephen's Green, Dublin 2, Ireland (a division of Penguin
Books Ltd.) • Penguin Group (Australia), 250 Camberwell Road, Camberwell, Victoria 3124, Australia
(a division of Pearson Australia Group Pty. Ltd.) • Penguin Books India Pvt. Ltd., 11 Community
Centre, Panchsheel Park, New Delhi—110 017, India • Penguin Group (NZ), 67 Apollo Drive,
Rosedale, Auckland 0632, New Zealand (a division of Pearson New Zealand Ltd.) • Penguin Books
(South Africa) (Pty.) Ltd., 24 Sturdee Avenue, Rosebank, Johannesburg 2196, South Africa

Penguin Books Ltd., Registered Offices: 80 Strand, London WC2R 0RL, England

While the author has made every effort to provide accurate telephone numbers, Internet addresses, and
other contact information at the time of publication, neither the publisher nor the author assumes any
responsibility for errors, or for changes that occur after publication. Further, the publisher does not have
any control over and does not assume any responsibility for author or third-party websites or their content.

First edition: July 2012

Library of Congress Cataloging-in-Publication Data

Unell, Amy E.
Starting at the finish line : coach Al Buehler's timeless wisdom / Amy E. Unell
with Barbara C. Unell and Bob Unell.
p. cm.
ISBN 978-0-399-53756-1
1. Buehler, Al. 2. Track and field coaches—United States—Biography. 3. Track and field—Philosophy.
4. Duke University—Track and field—Miscellanea. I. Unell, Barbara C., 1951– II. Unell, Bob. III. Title.
GV697.B85U54 2012 2012011753
796.42092—dc23 [B]

PRINTED IN THE UNITED STATES OF AMERICA

10 9 8 7 6 5 4 3 2 1

Most Perigee books are available at special quantity discounts for bulk purchases for sales
promotions, premiums, fund-raising, or educational use. Special books, or book excerpts,
can also be created to fit specific needs. For details, write: Special Markets, Penguin
Group (USA) Inc., 375 Hudson Street, New York, New York 10014.

For Coach Al and Delaina Buehler,
for always taking good care of those you love.

CONTENTS

CONTENTS

FOREWORD

Early in my freshman year at Duke, on a day when I was feeling fairly overwhelmed by my academic load as well as the requirements of playing Division I basketball for Mike (Coach K) Krzyzewski, I ran into Coach Al Buehler while walking to practice. He stopped me right outside Cameron Indoor Stadium, introduced himself as Duke's track coach, and encouraged me to hang in there. He said he had heard I was a great prospect for Duke and he conveyed his expectation of my success and his certainty that I would be okay.

Little did he know how important those words were to me at that particular time. It was exactly what I needed to pull me back into reality and get me to concentrate on what needed to be done—on the court as well as in the classroom.

Two years later, my roommate, Tony Lang, and I took Coach Buehler's class, History and Issues of Sports. In a small seminar setting of only nine or ten students, he taught us the rich history of sports in this country and the ethical way to approach any competition. Besides the course curriculum, this class also gave us insight into the man himself: his personality, his character, and his philosophy of life. As a teacher, he was fair and easygoing; he invited debate and disagreement. The course was stimulating and interesting, as well as richly informative.

But his seminar did not focus on his considerable contributions to track and field or to sport in general. It did not reveal his personal body of work that has made sport better today—more inclusive, more available to new athletes, more challenging for anyone who plays. It was not until I became involved as executive producer and narrator of the documentary *Starting at the Finish Line: The Coach Buehler Story* that I came to know the depth of his character, the important contributions he made to changing track and field, and the impact he had on so many well-known athletes, past and the present.

Through this book, inspired by the documentary, you will get a clear picture of the total man. I hope you will appreciate his value not only to Duke and Durham but also to countless students, both athletes and non-athletes, as well as to world-class Olympians and the entire Olympic movement. You will read the words of iconic Olympic greats such as Jackie Joyner-Kersee, Carl Lewis, Mary Decker Slaney, Joan Benoit Samuelson, and John Carlos as they speak about the effect Coach Buehler had on their lives, often at a critical moment in competition or in the aftermath of a win or loss.

Coach Buehler has taught me so much and enriched my life in ways it is hard to express. For me, the greatest lesson has been to show me how to conduct myself as an athlete and as a citizen of the world. He continues to make an important impact on the way I live my life and for that I am forever grateful.

—GRANT HILL
Seven-Time NBA All-Star
Two-Time NCAA Champion

THE MEANING OF "COACH"

I hope that I live and love life as much as Al Buehler. I think one of the reasons he's never grown old is that he loves to learn. You know that expression, when you stop learning, you stop living? This guy is about eighteen right now.

He drives this little yellow car, and when I see it, either in the parking lot or on the road, I smile. And I'll tell you what, that little yellow car is usually parked earlier than most of the people who come to work at Duke. And it usually stays later. And the reason is, he has never worked a day in his life; but he's lived every day of his life doing what he loves.

My players over the years have loved being in Al's class, and I've loved having them in Al's class. Whenever my players took his class, I told them to get to know him. I think he's got great integrity. He stands tall. His value structure makes him as tall as anybody on our campus. Become Al Buehler's friend, and you'll have a friend for life.

Paul Bollman (left) and Jess Peter (center) with Coach Buehler after the 1957 ACC Championships.

Mike (Coach K) Krzyzewski chats with his longtime friend and colleague Coach Al Buehler and former player Grant Hill during a photo shoot for the documentary *Starting at the Finish Line: The Coach Buehler Story*.

To me, Al is the best example of a teacher-coach in intercollegiate sports. He defines the word "coach." He set a standard for all of us to follow.

—MIKE (COACH K) KRZYZEWSKI
Olympic and Four-Time NCAA Championship Coach

1. TALK'S CHEAP
2. ACTIONS SPEAK
   LOUDER THAN WORDS
   "RESULTS".

INTRODUCTION

On the first day of spring semester classes in January, students enrolled in PE 49S, History and Issues of Sports, shuffle into room 101 of Cameron Indoor Stadium. Most of them are varsity athletes, and the football players and wrestlers among them somehow manage to maneuver their bodies and over-sized backpacks into the tight space crammed with plastic chairs, a creaky wooden bench, bronze trophies, DVDs, a sofa that's older than the president of the United States, and stacks and stacks of sports-related periodicals.

This is the office of Al Buehler, a middle-distance track star at the University of Maryland who came to Duke in 1955 to coach cross-country. Since then, he has become as legend-ary as football coach Wallace Wade, from whom he inherited the hand-me-down sofa. Plaques and posters cover nearly every inch of wall space, attesting to Buehler's impact on both Duke and the international track-and-field community.

Coach's classroom, Room 101 Cameron Indoor
Stadium, where he teaches the Duke undergraduate
class History and Issues of Sports. 2012.

He led Blue Devil track squads to six ACC championships; was elected president of the NCAA Track and Field Coaches Association in 1970; arranged for Duke to host the USSR-USA International Meet in 1974 and the USA–Pan Africa–Federal Republic of Germany Meet in 1975; served as team manager for U.S. Olympic track-and-field teams in Munich (1972), Los Angeles (1984), and Seoul (1988); and was head manager for the U.S. contingent at the World Indoor Championships in 2001. Yet his accomplishments off the track are equally remarkable. Buehler has a record of being attuned not just to sports imperatives but to cultural shifts—quietly promoting interracial sporting events as civil rights protests took place across the country and giving up all of his men's track scholarships so that Duke could offer athletic scholarships to women the year Title IX was enacted.

Today, Buehler maintains his lean runner's frame. Even though he officially retired from coaching in 2000, he continues to teach this intro course, which has attracted the likes of basketball standouts Grant Hill and Shane Battier. Chances are that most of the students in the class—young enough to be Buehler's grandchildren—don't know much about his legacy. No matter. Buehler tells them that he wants them to walk away from his class every day having learned something. "If I see blank faces," he says, looking around the room, "I'll know I've failed."

But he's also quick to impress upon them that they are responsible for their own learning. In the weeks to come, he says, he'll call on them to speak extemporaneously about a sports-related subject in the news, and the final oral exam will be "eyeball to eyeball, so I'll know pretty quickly whether you know about the quest for racial equality in sports."

"You are all starting off with one hundred points," he says in his raspy voice. "It's yours to blow."

As Buehler reviews the syllabus and distributes the course textbook, ESPN's *SportsCentury*, he begins to tell stories, weaving together his encyclopedic knowledge of Duke's history with references and context that the students in his class can grasp. He starts with a fantastic tale that unfolds in the early 1930s, when a fledgling Duke University was able to lure Alabama's Wade, the best football coach in the country, to Durham. "He was the Mike Krzyzewski of his time," says Buehler. (The next week he takes the class to the Football Hall of Fame in the Yoh Football Center, where the students seem genuinely surprised by the heights that the football program reached long before they were born: the undefeated and unscored-upon Iron Dukes team of 1938, the multiple bowl-game appearances, the long roster of All-Americans, the consecutive winning seasons.)

In the course of that first hour-and-fifteen-minute class, Buehler touches on the themes that will guide the semester—

the evolution of American sports from amateur exercises into a star-making, big-money machine; how the advent of televised sporting events changed the game; the impact of desegregation, Title IX, doping scandals, and NCAA regulations; and the role of athletics in higher education. It's a lot of ground to cover, and it's important, he says, because today's student-athletes need to understand the history of the landscape they find themselves in. And someday, he tells them, they may find themselves on the Duke board of trustees and be faced with critical, complicated decisions involving athletics.

But that's only a small part of his motivation for continuing to teach this class. At heart, Buehler is a mentor. Since his arrival on a campus still segregated by race and gender, he has outlasted six Duke presidents, become a father and a grandfather, battled a benign brain tumor that's affected his hearing and balance, had a Duke cross-country trail named for him, and coached thousands of young runners, including twelve All-Americans and five Olympians. Yet the majority of people in Buehler's generations of admirers include alumni who never went pro, but instead incorporated his worldview into their lives. In October 2011, at an advance screening of *Starting at the Finish Line: The Coach Buehler Story*, a documentary film produced and directed by Amy Unell, one of his former History and Issues of Sports students, hundreds of alumni and friends gave Buehler a standing ovation as the final credits rolled in Griffith Film Theater. (Grant Hill is narrator and one of the executive producers.)

For now, the students in PE 49S seem oblivious to the fact that the man standing before them genuinely cares more about their character than whether they grasp the pivotal role Curt Flood played in paving the way for athletes to become free agents or how controversial boxer Jack Johnson helped set the stage for Muhammad Ali. As Buehler wraps up the first day's class, a young woman asks for clarification about the following week's homework assignment. The football players sitting on Wallace Wade's old couch look at one another blankly when Buehler instructs students to write down their personal goals for the class.

Buehler turns his students' attention to a Latin phrase he has written on a flip chart.

"*Esse Quam Videri*," he says. " 'To be, rather than to seem.' I want you to write that down. You know what that means? Don't be a phony."

—Adapted from "*Esse Quam Videri*:
The Enduring Influence of Al Buehler," by Bridget Booher,
Duke Magazine, March–April 2011.
Reprinted by permission of *Duke Magazine*.

COACH'S NOTE

I like to think of myself as a teacher who happens to specialize in track and field. That's what coaching really is—it's teaching. Basically I am concerned with the overall development of my athletes and students. How high they jump or how fast they run is not nearly as important as what kind of person they turn out to be. I want them to be good husbands, fathers, wives, mothers, sons, daughters, and first-rate citizens.

For decades, my students and athletes have gotten a kick out of the racing spikes that hang from a bronze trophy sitting on the windowsill in my classroom at Cameron Indoor Stadium. I wore these spikes in 1952 during my last year running for Coach Jim Kehoe. I stuck a piece of tape in my spikes on which I wrote the words: WHY. REMEMBER. RACE PLAN. Whenever I put my foot in the shoe and felt that tape, it would remind me to go through that simple checklist. That

The original handwritten tape that Coach Buehler inserted inside his 1952 racing spikes to lead him to victory while running for the University of Maryland.

frayed piece of yellow tape with my handwritten words is still there today, some sixty years later.

WHY. At the beginning of each race, I'd ask myself: Why am I doing this? My answer: Because I like competing. I enjoy doing it. I had to remind myself, just like I remind my students today, to keep this rationale in my head.

REMEMBER. I wanted to remember all of the days when it was cold outside, and I had run my best, regardless of the weather. I had to remind myself that there is no excuse for not doing my best.

RACE PLAN. When we warmed up before the race, I'd get all hopped up. I had to remind myself that I still had to run the race, to follow the race plan.

These three ideas have guided me in my marriage, fatherhood, career, and faith. I tell my students and athletes: Remind yourself why you're doing what you're doing; remember that you can survive hard challenges because you have had to do so before; and follow the race plan, regardless of how anxious, excited, or worried you are.

My folks lived through the Great Depression. They lost their home and their jobs and had to sell apples for a nickel on street corners. I'm sure that's where I learned that you have to pay the price, usually in time, money, or effort. I am not talking about buying an expensive car or house; I'm talking about earning something through hard work and focusing on a goal. There are never any shortcuts. If you want to be a champion, you get up in the morning when you'd rather sleep in. You push yourself a little extra to make sure that you pay a greater price than your opponent will pay.

I have always believed that you need to set up your own race. Select a pace that is comfortable for you. Know your position in the race at all times. Be conscious of your form. Don't just plod along. *Think.* This is the secret.

Races, as a metaphor for all journeys, are usually decided on the hills, for the advantage gained there can never be overcome on the flat stretches. I would tell my athletes to be confident of your ability to blast up those hills.

The same can be said for running downhill. Naturally, your speed will increase, but it must be kept in check so that you're not running full tilt without control. Watch your footing at all times, as loose gravel can cause dangerous slides or spills.

In life, you see, there are uphill climbs and downhill slides. You have to have the mental conditioning to know how to navigate both. And that takes discipline and hard work, both of which come from deep inside. No one can do it for you.

I've been thinking about finish lines my entire life. I believe finish lines are something to prepare for; and in my world, they should be a place not of endings, but of beginnings. In my view of life, the finish line is a starting point . . . for dreams, for opening long-closed doors, for challenges . . . for change. Starting at the finish line also means carrying your principles and values forward beyond the finish line of any race or goal and into how you live your life.

I've always asked myself: What do I believe in? What do I put stock in and how do I follow that path? The answers are found in the Coachables described in each chapter in this book. They are the stuff that I'm the most proud of. And when I say proud, I don't mean boastful. I mean that I am proud to spend my time as a teacher and coach having fun passing on these words of wisdom to my students and athletes, as well as trying to model them for my children, Bo and Beth, and my grandchildren, Julia, Ruthie, and Will.

The best decision that I ever made was marrying my wife of over fifty years, Delaina. I often say to her, "Can you believe a little girl from Burlington, North Carolina, and a boy from Hagerstown, Maryland, have done all the things we have done?" and she always says, "No, I'm amazed."

—COACH AL BUEHLER

STARTING AT THE FINISH LINE

ONE

Esse Quam Videri
(To Be, Rather Than to Seem)

Few are those who wish to be endowed with virtue rather than to seem so.

—CICERO, *ON FRIENDSHIP*

STARTING LINE WISDOM

Coach lives his life by being genuinely honest about who he is. And he uses the North Carolina state motto, *Esse Quam Videri*, to communicate to his athletes and students how important he believes it is to find one's own identity.

"If there's one thing I am faithful to, it's owning up to who I am," Coach notes, reflecting on the powerful influence of this Coachable in his own life. "This is me, rough spots and all. I have always played it straight. Never cheated. I might outsmart somebody, but I'm not going to cheat him. If you don't follow your principles, then that's being a phony."

Coach Buehler reviews the race plan with Duke's first female runner and two-time All-American Ellison Goodall at Wallace Wade Stadium.

THE RIGHT ADVICE AT THE RIGHT TIME

According to renowned psychologist Erik Erikson's eight stages of human development, it is developmentally appropriate for young college students to use this time in their lives to reflect on the ideas of self-actualization and determining, to paraphrase Shakespeare in *Hamlet*, how to be true to themselves. Up to the stage of adolescence, development mostly depends upon what is done to us. Going forward, development depends primarily upon what we do. And while adolescence is a stage that straddles childhood and adulthood, life is definitely getting more complex as we attempt to find our own identity, struggle with social interactions, and grapple with moral issues.

During adolescence it is our challenge to separate from our family of origin and become "members of a wider society," as Erikson puts it. "If we are unsuccessful in navigating through this stage," he wrote, "we will experience role confusion and upheaval." It was the "psychologist" in Coach that recognized the importance of his role in helping young men and women steer successfully through these choppy waters. (This is an analogy that would not be lost on Buehler, who has spent many hours manning his skipjack on the Chesapeake Bay.)

Coach helped his athletes establish a philosophy in life and ideals by which they could determine their own course through life. Ellison Goodall Bishop, the first woman to run track and cross-country at Duke, found that Coach's care for her was expressed by his being more than her track coach; he was her life coach. When she approached him about running at Duke even before the school had a women's track team, he realized that he could help her connect with "who she was," her true passion. He saw her as a young person trying to realize her destiny through running and gave her a chance to realize her dreams on the track.

Ellison recalls: "I have this dream sometimes that I'm running, and I'm running so effortlessly and so easily that my feet aren't touching the ground, and it's just this enormously empowering feeling. That's what running was like. That's what Coach helped me recognize and experience. That's the kind of coach he was. He showed me what I could do, who I could be, by helping me believe in myself."

GETTING PAST THE DRAMA

Carl Lewis, who was mentored by Coach, explains how Buehler helped him maintain his focus on his quest for four gold medals:

Carl Lewis lets out a yell as he crosses the finish line to give the American 400-meter relay team a world record and the Olympic gold medal for the event. It was Lewis's fourth gold medal, which equals the feat of the legendary Jesse Owens. Los Angeles, August 11, 1984.

The 1984 Olympics were almost surreal for me. I had just turned twenty-three and was the biggest star of the biggest sports event in the world. There was so much drama, being in Los Angeles on our home turf, the expectations of going for four gold medals. The constant media attention was something that none of us had ever experienced, including Coach Buehler, who had been around the Olympics for many years. Coach had to get us past all of this drama so that I could actually perform. The pressure was high, because I was the one who was expected to match Jesse Owens's accomplishment of winning four gold medals. Coach Buehler was a genuine person I could trust to encourage me to focus on being the best I could be at each event. He not only was qualified to coach but was also a mentor and educator.

Although not directly coached by Buehler, Olympian Mary Decker Slaney explains how important it was for her to be in touch with her true passion and her identity. In commenting on the legendary track-and-field milestones that she reached in the 1970s, she says: "I wasn't running because I wanted to be famous or to be popular or whatever. I was running and being successful because that's what was inside of me. I was finding this little niche that I was good at."

For Carl Lewis or Mary Decker Slaney or any number of

champions, following the path of their true identity led them to great success on the track. But for others, Coach included, those paths may be "roads less traveled," to paraphrase M. Scott Peck. Following the precept of "to be, rather than to seem" took Buehler down a most unexpected road through the segregated South.

FOLLOWING THEIR INSTINCTS

It was not until 1963 that the first African-American undergraduates entered Duke University. But beginning in the late 1950s, Al Buehler and Dr. LeRoy Walker, track coach for North Carolina Central (NCCU), the nation's first state-supported liberal arts college for African-American students, had heard about the star athletes at each other's schools. So Buehler and Walker made the unprecedented and controversial move to bring the athletes together to train at Duke, which at the time boasted better facilities.

"In our part of the country," recalls Dr. Walker, who went on to become an Olympic coach and president of the U.S. Olympic Committee, "unless you had blinders on, it was not very difficult to see that I was from North Carolina Central and Al was from Duke. But Al and I never talked about the race issue. We were not there to get our names in the paper.

"We were like one person on the Duke and NCCU campuses. The people who came to Duke knew they came to see Walker-Buehler. We wanted to make sure that whatever we did, that it represented not just North Carolina Central and Duke University, but the sport.

"Duke had a superior track at Wallace Wade Stadium. We had to dodge puddles at North Carolina Central. So we trained our teams at Duke together. We knew each other's skills and utilized them. Al was very good at the distance runs, and he gave me the task of dealing with sprints and relays. We each

Legends of the sport and best friends LeRoy Walker and Al Buehler. 1975.

had Olympic athletes on our teams. Al had many superstars at Duke in events I didn't, and vice versa. Our strengths as coaches also were a good fit, as we could learn from each other.

"At this time in the South, Al and I couldn't drink from the same drinking fountain or eat with our teams at the same table at a restaurant. There were a lot of people who stopped going to those places to eat. We didn't put up strike signs, you know. We were together in what we were trying to accomplish. Al and I knew the problem, and we looked it right in the face. We focused on the fact that it's an 'us' picture, so let's make sure that it's 'us' representing these two universities. Al would not go to a meet that would not accept me."

Finish Line Wisdom

DETERMINE HOW YOU WANT TO LIVE.

Act in accordance with the values
that really matter to you.

BE HONEST ABOUT WHO YOU ARE.

"If you don't follow your principles,
then that's being a phony."

FOLLOW THE PATH OF YOUR TRUE IDENTITY.

Be true to yourself even if it means
you may take the "road less traveled."

TWO

Take Good Care of Those You Love

> He was always encouraging and motivating, always as your friend. He wanted us to do better, not just for him, not just for the team, not just for Duke, but for yourself as well. He helped you feel proud of yourself, even when you didn't succeed that day.
>
> —TOM MENAKER, ACC CHAMPIONSHIP TEAM

STARTING LINE WISDOM

The stories in this book focus on a coach who is unabashedly proud of his loving relationships between himself and his athletes, family, and students, a coach who knows the importance of showing that you care and knows how the simplest demonstration of caring can have profound inspirational effects on a person's life.

Coach Al Buehler is just the kind of man who not only has put his loving way of conducting himself into practice with unparalleled success but also has codified it as one of his key Coachables—the many aphorisms that he shared with the athletes with whom he came in contact, students in his classroom at Duke University, and with his family and friends.

Coach Buehler with Ed Stenberg, one of Duke's top long-distance runners of the late 1960s.

He proved that infusing his coaching, teaching, and parenting with love and respect can lead to producing not only outstanding athletes but also responsible people who reach their fullest potential.

It is timely and wise to look inside Buehler's coaching notebook and see why and how caring for others informed every aspect of Coach's life—and every Coachable in this book. The essential message here is this: When you care about others, you help them succeed. So it's no wonder that he writes this Coachable in all capital letters on the board that he's used for decades in the locker room and in the classroom:

TAKE GOOD CARE OF THOSE YOU LOVE

Dave Wottle, Olympic gold medalist, learned this Coachable on the track preparing for the biggest race of his life. "Coach Buehler would say, 'You can do it. You're ready to go,'" Wottle said, referring to his coach's words of encouragement. "It made me feel confident that I had him as my go-to person at the Olympics. He was always there for me. Sounds like a simple thing, but it's not. Having a support base there means a lot to an athlete when you're going into competition. I remember him getting with me and saying, "Dave, I'm here to do whatever you want me to do. If you want me to just keep split times in your workouts, I can do that. You tell me what you want."

UNCONDITIONAL LOVE

Coach Buehler readily admits that the hard part is putting those words into action—and living by them. But by every account, Coach Buehler does so—in the classroom today, as well as at home, in his neighborhood, and in his community. As the testimonies in this book will confirm, Coach has been a teacher, mentor, father figure, and more to countless people during his nearly sixty-year career. He not only left a lasting impression on so many but helped them cope with the challenges—and successes—in sports, at school, and in their personal lives. From the Olympians to passing acquaintances, he created a personal relationship with each person who came within his circle. At the center of that relationship was Coach Buehler's unconditional love.

Taking good care of those he loves is Coach's top priority, and his respect for "those in his care" has always guided him. And in return, his athletes, students, friends, and family lifted Coach up, especially when he needed them most when he was diagnosed with a benign brain tumor. Every day for several weeks before and after his surgery, he received a card or phone call from one or another athlete or former student checking in on him. He had been there for each of them when they needed his support, and now it was each one's turn to take good care of the man who they simply called "Coach." And they did.

At a reunion of Duke's track and cross-country teams after his surgery, the team members had tears of relief and joy in their eyes, as they gathered in his living room and reminisced about how Coach's love for them helped them reach their athletic *and* personal potential. Their emotions were fueled not only by their gratitude that their beloved friend and mentor was recovering so well but also by their happiness over their memories of the profound difference that his caring had made in their lives. They spoke about how he was like a second loving father, who had taught them to put others' well-being ahead of their own by his example of showing selfless and unreserved concern for them.

IT'S ALL ABOUT THE KIDS

Staley Gentry, a former member of Duke's cross-country team, recounted his discussions with Coach during his sophomore year about what Staley wanted to do with his life. Staley always thought that he would be a high school math teacher and coach, as both his parents were teachers. Coach's unequivocal advice: Staley needed to think about who he was and what *he* wanted to do, not just follow in his parents' footsteps. As simple as that sounds, Coach's advice changed his life and steered him in a new direction.

Decades after he graduated and visited Buehler, who was still actively teaching and coaching at the time, Staley asked him, "Coach, how can you do it? I mean, it's the same thing, year after year. And you've been doing this for forty-five years! I can still see you out there on the hill saying, 'You're coming to the hills, gotta be tough!'"

Coach's reply was typical: "It's all about the kids. The great thing about my job is every year there's a new crop coming in and I do whatever I can do to have influence on their lives.'"

Staley, who today is retired from leading a national financial services company, is the first to admit that Coach is the single most influential person in his life. He said, "Anything I needed to talk about, any pain that I was going through, all I had to do is go talk to Coach. And he took it like it was his own. He was like my dad. In fact, he was probably much closer to me than my dad."

FOLLOW YOUR HEART

Dave Wottle had a similar experience. Just prior to the 1972 Olympics, Head Olympic and University of Oregon Track

Coach Bill Bowerman strongly urged Wottle not to get married before the games because he thought it would hinder his performance. Buehler, who was then a member of the Olympic coaching staff, saw it differently. He encouraged Wottle to follow his heart and believed that doing so would be a positive force in the end. And it was. Wottle took home the gold in the 800 meters.

Everyone within Coach's circle looked to him as a leader who cared about more than performance at a track meet or on a test. He wanted every athlete and student to perform for him in response to his empathy, the root of all caring. He truly came to understand each person's strengths and weaknesses and was able to guide them to their fullest potential.

BECOMING A TRUE CHAMPION

Duke University's legendary men's basketball coach, Mike (Coach K) Krzyzewski, recognizes Coach Buehler's capacity to empathize, to get into a student's heart and mind. "Al Buehler's worked with some of the greatest athletes in the world, studying their training techniques, getting to know them," he says. "He's been able to figure out not just how to high-jump or to run, but why somebody would put in an extra bit of practice, the mental stuff that goes along. For him, this is the most important part of becoming a champion."

Coach's caring about the emotional health of his athletes is evident in virtually every decision that he's made, even those which may not have seemed so helpful to those involved at the time. For Al Joyner, it was as simple as selecting a roommate during his participation at the Olympic Games in 1984.

"I wanted to room with my friend and former roommate at previous contests, Mike Conley," says Joyner. "But Coach had another idea. He said that he knew that we were best friends, but this was the Olympic Games. Being in separate rooms would allow each of us to focus on achieving our best performance.

"I didn't understand it at the time. But I took his advice anyway and ended up rooming with Carl Lewis and Kirk Baptiste. To this day, I would say that Coach Buehler's advice was vitally important to my winning a gold medal. He was looking out for both Conley and me. As it turned out, Conley was the favorite at the time. There was a newspaper report that had just been published about the top contenders to win the triple jump at the Olympics. He was mentioned, but I wasn't. I was upset after reading that and went back to my room. If Conley and I had been roommates, I probably would have gotten myself worked up complaining to him. Because Coach showed me that it's all about how you set your mind, I was able to digest that article, *by myself in my own room*, which helped to motivate me even more. I was okay."

America's Al Joyner, who won gold in the triple jump, raises the hand of his sister, Jackie, who won silver in the women's heptathlon. Los Angeles, 1984.

WORDS OF WISDOM AND REASON

Olympian Jackie Joyner-Kersee has never forgotten the difference that Coach's friendship made in her life just when she needed someone she could depend on to help her physically, spiritually, and emotionally.

"When a person cares about you, he gives you words of encouragement. And those words can feel like pure wisdom. As one of my Olympic coaches in 1984 and 1988, Coach provided words of reason that comforted my fellow athletes and me.

"I was twenty-two years old, and Los Angeles was my first Olympic Games. I didn't know what to expect because everything was overwhelming. Coach knew that the Olympic Village could be like Las Vegas, so he encouraged me to maintain my focus. He reminded me that I could have fun, but I still had a job to do. Because he cared about me personally, he made sure I stayed hydrated, wore a hat (of course, he wore his trademark straw hat all the time!), and stayed out of the sun when I could. He also emphasized the importance of getting my rest and attending team meetings. They were the things that you can easily take for granted, but they made a big difference.

"I was competing in multiple events in the 1984 Olympic

Games for two days straight. I was injured, as well, so I was doing a lot of physical therapy work. I was in so much pain that I thought the world was coming to an end. Just when I needed him, Coach was there, motivating me to do my very best, giving me the encouragement I really needed. It would put me at ease just to see him smile.

"Coach Buehler is quiet, but when he speaks, he speaks volumes."

THE IMMEASURABLE VALUE OF CARING

Like Al Joyner and countless others, Coach's daughter, Beth, says she could never put a value on her father's caring for her. "My father's love," she says, "has kept me grounded, centered, my entire life."

Coach Buehler believes that teaching children to be loving, caring people starts with his own behavior. "Don't expect them to do something if you're not willing to do so yourself," he says about how he and his wife, Delaina, raised Beth and their son, Bo. Coach's parenting, coaching, and teaching styles were all the same—rooted in love for those in his care.

Experts in child development and education know that a child's first and most important teacher is his parent. Coach knew it, too. He says that he was lucky to have had that model of a "teaching" parent in his own mom and dad, who dem-

Coach Buehler with his mentor and coach Jim Kehoe of the University of Maryland.

onstrated that one doesn't motivate children by intimidating them to behave simply to avoid punishment, but teaches them by reinforcing their positive behavior. Coach Jim Kehoe, Buehler's own coach at the University of Maryland, motivated him on the track in the same way and was as much a "father" to him as a coach. These important people in Buehler's life were all caring, emotionally intelligent mentors who loved him unconditionally.

Of course, Coach would never refer to himself or anyone else as "emotionally intelligent." He didn't need the behavioral research by authors like Daniel Goleman or Stephen Covey to tell him that being trustworthy resulted in others knowing you cared about them. Or that caring for others can be more important in determining successful relationships in families, at work, in athletics, and in education, than any other factor.

In their book *Unto Others*, philosopher Elliott Sober and biologist David Sloan Wilson concluded that people with truly altruistic desires are "reproductively fitter than creatures without—altruists, in short, make better parents than do egoists." This commentary helps to explain why Coach's unselfish, empathic, and caring way of coaching and teaching worked so well in his personal life.

Commenting on their over five decades of marriage, Coach shares that he and Delaina still feel like they're courting. But he adds that taking care of those you love takes work: "You

Al and Delaina Buehler
on the day before
their wedding.
December 20, 1958.

can't just talk about it. You have to live it. If you don't stop
and appreciate the moment, the days can get all gobbled up."

Coach and Delaina start each morning and end each day
with a ten-second kiss. Why ten seconds? He explains, "That
gives you a long enough kiss to enjoy it. You get that spark.
It's one of those things that nature just works out," he adds
with a sheepish, classic Coach Buehler grin.

Finish Line Wisdom

EMPATHY IS THE ROOT OF ALL CARING.
When you put yourself in others' shoes,
you are able to support their strengths
and help them overcome their weaknesses.

SET AN EXAMPLE.
Teaching others to be loving, caring people starts
with your own behavior.
You can't expect anyone to do something
you're not willing to do.

LOVE TAKES WORK AND TIME.
Show you care by your words and actions.
The little things you do—listening, encouraging,
or giving a pat on the back—
make a big difference.

THREE

Be the Most Positive, Enthusiastic Person You Know

Coach was always up. Never down. Never saw him have a bad day, no matter what happened. He is just a very positive person.

—DAVE SIME, OLYMPIC SILVER MEDALIST

STARTING LINE WISDOM

It's no wonder that so many athletes who came in contact with Coach remember his enthusiasm. He thought it was the most important ingredient in coaching. "I don't know of any unenthusiastic coaches who were worth their salt," he says. "If you can't be excited about something, why should any of your students?"

As you come to know and develop your own true identity, you have the opportunity and the self-confidence to show the world who you are, acting on your beliefs as you pursue your hopes and dreams. Coach knows that when you let your beliefs guide you, you generate a genuine enthusiasm that can inspire and motivate those around you.

Sporting his trademark straw hat, Coach Buehler stands at the finish line at Duke's Wallace Wade Stadium. 1990.

For Buehler, "being the most positive enthusiastic person you know" is as much about *acting* enthusiastic as it is about feeling enthusiastic. When you believe in something, it's important to reveal that belief, unabashedly, in a positive way through your words and actions. Coach's success in track and field is a testament to his putting this belief into action.

NBA star and captain of the Duke NCAA Championship team in 2001, Shane Battier took Buehler's class when Coach was in his seventies. "Coach's class was a *fun* A," according to Battier. "It wasn't so much an easy A, as *fun*, which made it easy. It was one of those classes for which you actually liked doing the work. A lot of people go through their college experiences and don't remember their professors, or maybe don't recall what they learned in class. I can remember Coach Buehler's class like it was yesterday. I remember everything—even the classroom! The walls were lined with four decades of American sports memorabilia: team trophies, framed photos, and tarnished plaques.

"It's one thing to have a young professor talking about the history and development of sport," adds Battier, "but Coach Buehler lived it. It was cool to hear the firsthand experiences from his perspective."

BECOME THE CHANGE YOU WANT TO SEE

Coach Buehler believed deeply in the importance of all human beings living in harmony. He acted on this belief and let those around him know with a genuine enthusiasm that helped to change history. In doing so, Coach became a quiet trailblazer for many causes, breaking down barriers of race (in his collaboration with Dr. LeRoy Walker) and gender (as testified by his unreserved support for women's track at Duke and the Olympics that was a key in the advancement of the cause).

Joan Benoit Samuelson, Olympic gold medalist in 1984, remembers Coach's role as a trailblazer for women: "I think Coach Buehler had such a love of the sport that he wanted to instill that passion in his athletes. He had the foresight to realize that women can be athletes, too. And they can inspire and set great marks, just as men could, through sports."

LIVING LONGER STRONGER

Coach's enthusiasm not only powered the success of his athletes but may, in large part, account for his own longevity. In their review of dozens of research studies, "Positive Affect and Health," published in *Current Directions in Psychological*

Science, Sheldon Cohen and Sarah D. Pressman showed that positive emotions are associated with a range of better general health outcomes, from years of additional life to a decreased likelihood of catching the common cold.

And it shows in Coach's face every day. His eyes still light up when you ask him why he stayed in coaching so long and still teaches. "Because I enjoyed it," he states with a smile. "I haven't forgotten what it is like to be a student and get excited about something. I got up this morning and all I was thinking about was teaching my afternoon class! It reminds me of the anticipation of stepping on the track when I was really nervous. When you're excited about something, learning is so much easier."

ACHIEVING THE IMPOSSIBLE

Former Duke track star Robbie Perkins shares how Coach Buehler's enthusiasm and positive approach inspired him to achieve something he never thought would be possible.

"I will never forget the night before the ACC Championships when I was a sophomore at Duke. Coach called me up and said, 'Robbie you're going to run the mile *and* the 3 mile at the ACC Championships.' I spent the next couple of minutes trying to talk him out of having me run the mile because

I didn't consider myself much of a miler and I wanted to *win* the 3 mile.

" 'You know,' Coach responded, 'you ran a really good race up against the University of Richmond, and I think you can show really well at the mile. I'll worry about the 3 mile after you finish the mile.'

"So I was nervous and didn't sleep a wink that night. I got to the meet the next morning for the mile, figuring that I was probably the slowest person in the field. And then, with about two hundred yards to go, I had the lead. I came around the corner, and Coach Buehler was there screaming, 'Get going, get going!'

"All of a sudden, everybody in the stands started coming to their feet. I ran as hard as I could down the stretch and leaned into the tape. I ended up winning the ACC mile. *It was because Coach Buehler threw me in there!*

"As soon as I crossed the finish line, Coach came up, put his arm around me, and said, 'You have a chance to do something special tonight. I want you off your feet. You've got twenty-five minutes before the 3-mile race. You're going be the fastest guy because you're the ACC mile champion.'

"And sure enough, in the 3 mile, I said to myself, 'I'm the fastest guy on the track.' And I took off and won the race.

Coach Buehler did a brilliant job of getting my head right to do that.

"He was one of those guys who had the enthusiasm and the ability to put a group of talented runners together and coach them to another level. He's never going to get up in the morning without being optimistic about what's going to happen that day. If there is anyone who has a positive attitude toward everything every day, it is Coach Buehler. There is never a down moment with him.

"He had standards that we had to live up to or he wasn't going be happy. If there was ever somebody to bust yourself wide open for, it was Coach. I mean, he was an incredible motivator. He'll run a race until the day they close the door. He's just that kind of guy. He's never going to give up."

Finish Line Wisdom

LET YOUR BELIEFS GUIDE YOU.

By being true to yourself, you can generate
a genuine enthusiasm that will motivate you
and inspire those around you.

YOUR "JOB" IS TO HAVE A BENEFICIAL
INFLUENCE ON OTHERS.

Setting the standard—by your words and actions—
will make an immeasurable difference to your own
life as well as those around you.

POSITIVE EMOTIONS,
INCLUDING ENTHUSIASM,
ALWAYS LEAD TO POSITIVE OUTCOMES.

Every aspect of your life—
from reaching your own goals to coping well
with stresses to living longer and stronger—
is affected by your attitude.

FOUR

Be Bold and Courageous

Your time is limited, so don't waste it living someone else's life. Don't be trapped by dogma—which is living with the results of other people's thinking. Don't let the noise of others' opinions drown out your own inner voice. And most important, have the courage to follow your heart and intuition.

—STEVE JOBS

STARTING LINE WISDOM

Everything begins with the courage to believe in yourself and to have the courage of your convictions. It takes courage to take a stand—and at every turn Coach has encouraged boldness in his students and athletes—and lived and acted courageously himself.

THE COURAGE TO WALK AWAY; THE COURAGE TO RETURN

"At the 1972 Olympics in Munich, I was on the coaching staff for the track team. I was two hundred yards away from

U.S. athletes Tommie Smith (center) and John Carlos (right) extend their gloved fists skyward during the playing of "The Star-Spangled Banner" after Smith received the gold and Carlos the bronze for the 200-meter run at the Summer Olympic Games in Mexico City. Australia's silver medalist Peter Norman is at left. 1968.

the Athletes' Village when I heard the helicopters and saw the automatic machine guns," his story begins. Eight members of the Palestinian group Black September had stormed the Olympic Village and taken the Israeli athletes hostage. Later that day, he learned that all of the Israeli athletes, five of the terrorists, and one German police officer were killed.

Coach admits to feeling a sense of fear, disillusionment, and sorrow over losing the athletes to this violence—and knowing how the Games had been perverted by the killers to gain attention for their cause. To sort through his personal emotional upheaval after this experience, he had to take some time to reflect on what happened. For the next twelve years he did not participate in the Olympic program.

His return to Olympic coaching demonstrated how consistently Coach takes care of those he loves and showed that he has the moral courage to follow his heart. He came back to the Olympics first out of his love and obligation to his athletes and, perhaps equally important, he admits, to justify his own parents' pride in their son's accomplishments on the Olympic stage.

"I don't regret my decision," Coach says. "While it was hard for me to walk away, it was equally challenging to return. I'm glad I did both."

A track official attempts to comfort a crying Mary Decker after Decker's fall in the women's 3000-meter run at the Olympic Games. Los Angeles, August 10, 1984.

COURAGE TAKES MENTAL AND PHYSICAL TOUGHNESS

To be bold and courageous is as much about the heart and mind as it is about the body. It would have been easy for Mary Decker Slaney to stop following her heart at the 1984 Olympics when her body failed her.

"When I watch the race footage [from the 3000-meter final at the '84 Olympics], I see that my hand touched the back of my competitor, Zola Budd, and pulled her number off of her uniform," Mary recalls. "I honestly do not remember that. I do remember falling. It all happened so fast, like being in a car wreck or something. My Olympic dream was over."

She could have easily walked away from the Olympics forever. But instead, she picked herself up, dusted herself off, and started all over again, as the old song goes. She was so determined to prove to herself that she should have won in 1984 that she went undefeated in 1985. "I beat everybody convincingly. I broke the world record in the mile and broke most of the American records I already held. So it was my best year, performance-wise, ever. And even to this day, I don't think I would have had that kind of performance year had 1984 not happened the way it did. I believe you get something good out of everything bad. As the saying goes, 'you turn lemons into lemonade.'"

THE COURAGE TO BLAZE NEW TRAILS

Joan Benoit Samuelson, Olympic gold medalist, appreciates the courage of the group of women who came together to advance women's track and field. "We weren't the first generation of female runners, but we were right in on the heels of that first generation with Jacqueline Hansen and Miki

Gorman," she says. "We all understood how much effort and commitment and dedication goes into our sport".

Coach Buehler's first female athlete, Ellison Goodall Bishop, remembers the courageous acts—hers and Coach's—that launched her career in track and field.

"When I first saw Coach Al," remembers Bishop, "he was standing on the track, stopwatch in hand, talking to a small band of runners. It was the end of the season, when only those who would compete in the national championship were still training. I watched from the tunnel as the guys stood in a circle around him, listening to his directions. They were serious, but there was also a casual exchange of laughter and banter among them.

"I would end up walking through the tunnel two more times before I had the courage to go out on the track and introduce myself," she continues. "It must have taken some ridiculous surge of courage or insanity for me to even approach Al Buehler. I had never run on a track before and had only been jogging for a couple of years. I knew nothing about the sport, yet Coach Al responded to me with interest and sincerity. He asked me to run around the track. It seemed a simple request. Little did I know that he had opened a door that would change my life and lead me in a direction I never imagined possible."

Coach recognized that Ellison loved to run. And at the same time, Ellison's act of courage inspired Coach. She acted on her convictions that she could be part of the program at Duke if she was given a chance. He would make the bold decision to start training her, which led to the founding of the women's track program at Duke.

ONE ACT OF COURAGE BEGETS ANOTHER

Olympic gold medalist John Carlos revisits one of the most memorable moments in Olympic history when he and teammate Tommie Smith made a bold political statement courageously staging a civil rights demonstration on the medal stand of the 1968 Olympics.

"When I needed someone to be there, God sent Al Buehler. And I believe that he sent him for a reason.

"Tommie Smith and I were gold and bronze medalists, respectively, in the 200-meter race at the 1968 Olympic Games in Mexico City. As we stood on the medal stand, the American flag was raised and the national anthem was played. Tommie and I bowed our heads and put our fists to the sky, as a silent protest against racial discrimination.

"I remember everyone applauding vigorously at first; then people realized that we were doing something very much out of the norm, and they felt threatened by it. Any time you feel threatened about something, the result is anger. That's what happened, and sunshine turned to rain, so to speak.

"People started booing. They started hissing. As we left the victory stand, people were shouting the 'n' word and spitting at us and throwing things. They were screaming, 'You need to go back to Africa,' and all kinds of stuff like that. There was madness going on everywhere. Then we were booted out of the Olympic Village.

"And then there was Al Buehler. He took it upon himself to give us a ride to the airport. He gave us moral support by letting us know that we did a courageous thing, had nothing to be ashamed of, and should feel good about ourselves. He told me that what we had done and the way we did it was very eloquent, with no violence involved. He told me that we had just made a statement that was pure and genuine, and in the long run, it was going to be accepted by all the people.

"He had such confidence about who we all were and what we had accomplished. He's always been there, never denied us or stepped back from us, or tried to make excuses for who we were and what we did. He just let us be who we were.

"Coach Buehler is as committed an individual to the sport of track and field as I have ever known. He showed me that he had love for humanity, not just by supporting what I did on the medal stand but also how he had a concern about bringing the races together in the sport he loves.

"He and LeRoy Walker were not looking at individuals as being white or black or rich or poor, but as young protégés that they could mold into being great Americans. They showed the world how people can come together, regardless of their ethnic background, to become a cohesive team, [to be] understanding and loving toward one another."

Finish Line Wisdom

IT TAKES COURAGE TO TAKE A STAND.

Let the world know who you are and
what you believe in, and risk the reaction
from others that might not be positive.

DON'T UNDERESTIMATE THE COURAGE
IT TAKES TO WALK AWAY.

It may take even more determination
to come back to it.

COURAGE TAKES MENTAL AS WELL
AS PHYSICAL TOUGHNESS.

It takes resoluteness to reflect objectively on
negative experiences—and boldness to take action
to turn them into something positive.

FIVE

Results, Not Excuses

Coach Buehler kept to the basics. There are no shortcuts.
Work hard, do it consistently, and good things will come
to you.

—ROBBIE PERKINS, ACC CHAMPION

STARTING LINE WISDOM

"Results, not excuses" is more than an axiom that Coach
spouted at practice or in the classroom. It was the motivator
he used with his athletes and students to demonstrate that he
cared about their success. This Coachable is an expression of
love because it says:

> When you love someone, you want him to be all he can
> be . . . you want him to find his own strength and power,
> and achieve the results in life that he wants.

"Results, not excuses" lifts us up and gets us back on a path
of problem-solving when adversity strikes. It forces us to focus

Four-time Southern Conference Champion for the
University of Maryland, a young Al Buehler (center)
sprints to the finish line. 1952.

on the positive ways to overcome obstacles and to reach our full potential. Coach's belief in the power of being "the most positive, enthusiastic person you know" informs this Coachable.

Buehler refused to accept excuses or negativity from his students and athletes or from himself; instead, he embraced challenges. With this conscious approach to life, he internalized this Coachable, and in doing so, helped everyone in his circle do so, too.

Mary Decker Slaney, Olympic gold medalist, saw firsthand how Coach's approach to life led to a remarkable boost in international relations. She first met Coach in 1974 at the USSR-USA International Track and Field Meet at Duke University's Wallace Wade Stadium in Durham. Mary recalls: "It was a *huge* meet. I was surprised that there was such a big outdoor meet in the United States involving the Russians, particularly at the height of the Cold War. But I quickly learned that this was really a testament to the dedication of Coach Al Buehler and Dr. LeRoy Walker, both of whom were fixtures in the track-and-field world." And, true to their shared philosophy of "results, not excuses," they brought the meet to Durham, North Carolina.

FOCUS ON THE GOAL AT HAND

Buehler admits that another underlying message inherent in this Coachable—to focus on the goal at hand—was demonstrated nowhere more intensely than when he and his friend LeRoy Walker were working together on the international track meets that would put Durham on the map.

At the height of racial tensions in the country in the 1960s, the two coaches went out in the community together to promote and plan their track meets, talking at churches, schools, clubs, business groups, and community organizations to get sponsors and volunteers. Both Buehler and Walker refused to let excuses stand in their way; instead, they focused on their goals, and modeled racial harmony and mutual respect between two stellar athletic programs. And the people of Durham bought into it. Remarkably, it was how Buehler and Walker went about getting support—more like parents promoting their athletic programs, than as sports coaches, per se—that won people over.

BE RESPONSIBLE

At the heart of this Coachable is this truth: It is better to embrace your challenges and own up to your responsibilities than it is to remain helpless, hopeless, and hapless. Cognitive behavioral research demonstrates that the latter "poor me" victim mentality can lead to depression, create a sense of anxiety, and inhibit problem-solving, all of which keep you from achieving the best results.

More than 52,000 people attended the Pan Africa–USA International Meet, a historic event marking the first time all of the African nations ran under one flag. July 16–17, 1971.

EARN WHAT YOU GET

The threads of this Coachable run deep into Coach's childhood. He says that his parents never wanted all As on his report cards. But when he got a C, it alarmed them that he wasn't performing up to his highest potential.

"They'd ask what was happening to make me get a C in Algebra," he recounted. "'If you don't understand Algebra, get help to learn it,' they'd say. They expected me to move forward in school, and the only way to do so was by making sure that I was learning what was being taught. Have you heard the saying, 'There's no free lunch'? That's what my parents were really saying. You have to do the work. You have to earn what you get in life."

As do all loving parents, Coach's mother and father had two challenges: helping their child learn the skills he needed to master the subject, as well as learn how to problem-solve instead of making excuses when he wasn't able to reach his goal. While the immediate goal for the young Al was to improve his grade in Algebra, in truth, doing well in school was simply a rehearsal for meeting all challenges in life, big and small.

And so it was with Coach and his students and athletes. He was a great champion of "continuing education" who encouraged his charges to keep on learning new coping skills.

And by his example, he provided an important ingredient in their lives that made them more resilient and emotionally healthy.

TALK IS CHEAP: ACTIONS SPEAK LOUDER THAN WORDS

When Buehler first came to Duke University, he motivated his new team by simply showing them that he could outperform them all. He saw that they were out of shape and wanted to inspire them to get stronger. "I figured the best way to do that was to demonstrate that they could achieve good results from the practice routines I was giving them," he says, "I told them that I had put myself on the same routine, and then showed the results."

Two-time ACC champion Robbie Perkins recalls: "He simply had a lot of spark to him. I remember the day when he said, 'You guys just aren't strong enough,' and then he went over to the pull-up bar and did fifteen pull-ups. Everybody was going, 'Oh, we can't do that, Coach!'" From that time on, the fifteen pull-ups required in every team practice came to be known by Coach as the "Buehler Fifteen," and within six weeks, everyone on the team had the routine down pat.

PUT YOUR MONEY WHERE YOUR MOUTH IS

It had always been Coach's conviction that women should have the same right to compete in track and field as the men. And when he was Duke's assistant athletic director, he took some pretty drastic action to make it possible by giving up his track scholarships the first year that Title IX was in place. He wanted track to be a model for other sports at Duke—and for all college sports in the country.

Tom Butters, former athletic director at Duke, remembers when universities were implementing the new Title IX, the landmark legislation that bans sex discrimination in schools, whether it be in academics or athletics. University budgets now had to make room for women's sports.

"I called Coach into the office one day," Butters recollects, "and told him I had made a decision, and that it was a firm decision: His men's track-and-field scholarships were gone, due to reallocation of our budget. He wasn't the only coach who lost scholarships. And he accepted it as gracefully as a man could without any show of emotion whatsoever. He simply accepted it and said, 'If that's what's good for the team, then that suits me.' "

Finish Line Wisdom

**DON'T LET OBSTACLES—
OF YOUR MAKING OR OTHERS'—
KEEP YOU FROM REACHING YOUR FULL POTENTIAL.**

Turn your attention on those positive things that
enable you to be the best you can be.

FOCUS ON THE GOAL AT HAND.

Don't let yourself be distracted from the path
of reaching your goal, even if it means taking
the occasional detour to achieve your end.

**VICTIM THINKING CAN ONLY LEAD
TO ANXIETY, PROCRASTINATION, BLAMING,
AND DEPRESSION.**

Take responsibility.
Only you can determine the course of your life.

KEEP LEARNING.

Problem-solving doesn't end when you leave school.
Always be open to acquiring new skills
to navigate through life's ups and downs.

**TALK IS CHEAP.
ACTIONS SPEAK LOUDER THAN WORDS.**

To encourage others and to keep
yourself motivated, what you do is infinitely
more important that what you say.

HAVE THE COURAGE OF YOUR CONVICTIONS.

Take action, even when all the odds
seem to be against you.

SIX

Inch by Inch, Everything's a Cinch

Duke wasn't known as a track power. But Coach said that
we have a chance to build something here. And that was a
challenge for me. I wanted to go someplace where I could
make my mark, instead of just joining a power that was
already established.

—BOB WHEELER,
OLYMPIAN, NCAA CHAMPION, THREE-TIME ALL-AMERICAN

STARTING LINE WISDOM

It would stand to reason that someone who is tone deaf would
be thought foolish to try to learn to play the bell chimes in his
church—and most especially, keep playing them at the age
of eighty. But neither his lack of musical training nor the fact
that the bells were located one hundred feet above the ground
atop a winding stairway were insurmountable obstacles for
Al Buehler. His son, Bo, did give voice to what many were
thinking: "We thought he was crazy! He couldn't carry a tune
in a bucket! But that was Dad, never letting a challenge stop
him if he believed that it was the right thing to do."

Coach felt deeply that his church was at the core of his
spiritual life. So when the church's bell ringer, who was

Olympian Bob Wheeler (left), a three-time
All-American and NCAA Champion, with Coach
Al Buehler. Early 1970s.

retiring, was looking for a volunteer to take his place, Coach literally and figuratively heeded the call! And once he took up the challenge, he just figured that he would learn how to play this instrument in the same way he'd always taken on new things (and the way he'd encouraged his athletes and students to excel)—inch by inch.

Coach's will to succeed in this was ignited by his determination to always be "bold and courageous" (which shows just how intertwined his Coachables are). And while he wasn't putting his life on the line (unless you consider the steep climb up the stairs of the bell tower to be life-threatening), it was either bold and courageous or hotheaded and reckless for a tone-deaf individual to continue to take on this role of church bell ringer at an age when most people would content themselves with collecting the weekly offering from the congregation.

Coach gave himself and his students permission to try and fail, get up and try again, take it slow, not be in a hurry, and apply singular focus to whatever goal they set out to reach. And his inch-by-inch thinking allowed him to reach this goal. Coach practiced what he preached, literally, whether it was the bells or the mile run. He started off by mastering just one song. It took him six months to learn how to pace himself with the notes and the music, but as his confidence grew, so did his skill and memory.

Every Sunday for thirty-five years, he literally inched his way up the narrow passageway, slow and steady, all by himself, negotiating the final ascent on a twenty-foot rickety wooden ladder and defying all the odds to send the glorious and joyful sound of those bells over the city of Durham.

Following a similar pattern of starting small and building his track program, inch by inch, Coach recalls how he put together his first team:

My first year coaching at Duke, I didn't even have the minimum of seven kids for a cross-country team. I went to the admissions office and asked them to give me the names of any students who were interested in track and field. I had to recruit guys out of the dorm, knock on doors, and ask if they wanted to join the team. I sent penny postcards to all of the coaches who had state champions in high school to get the word out that Duke had a cross-country team.

In that first year, we only beat one team, Wake Forest. The second year, with some of those kids from our first year team who returned, we beat Wake Forest *twice*. You could now say we were twice as good. I figured if my alma mater, Maryland, and my old coach, Jim Kehoe, could have a solid program, why can't we do the same thing at Duke? The third year, we won the conference. And thereafter, we had a stretch of twelve out of thirteen years when we either won it or were second, a winning streak that resulted in six ACC Championships, the most of any coach at Duke in the 1970s.

Inch by inch, Coach built his team, instilling in every player the same determination, enthusiasm, patience, and courage that kept him going. He knew that he had to put time and energy into his team building, or it would never be possible to reach his goals.

"It wasn't just the players who needed to get better," he admits. "I was learning how to coach better, too."

The late Duke and Olympic athlete Bob Wheeler once complained to his relay teammates, "Don't put me down thirty yards and expect me to win it for you guys. Your job is to keep it close, and then I'll win it for you." Wheeler was comparing each leg of the race to an "inch." He understood that you couldn't ignore the early steps and just focus on the final step if you wanted to win the race. Slowly but surely, the race will be won when each relay team member takes care of his "inch" of the race. He had learned "inch-by-inch" thinking and was passing it along to his teammates, a tribute to Coach, and the consummate honor for this teacher on the playing field of sports and life.

A PLAN TO MOVE FORWARD

No matter what task you undertake, you need a plan. And this Coachable reminds us that every good plan has clear and achievable markers along the way. With inch-by-inch thinking, you're going to set smaller goals that will eventually lead you to your ultimate goal. This measured approach will also give you points along the way where unforeseen challenges will test your resolve and help you determine whether the plan needs to be modified or your goal needs to be adjusted.

Coach used this planning technique with his athletes, helping each to form a strategy for every race, every season, and their entire lives. Every student and athlete that entered his classroom was reminded of this Coachable when they saw his old spikes with the frayed bit of tape on the inner sole on which he'd written the words: WHY. REMEMBER. RACE PLAN. And many of these young people have said that they have used inch-by-inch thinking throughout their lives and careers.

"You learn so many lessons from your time in athletics," says Olympic gold medalist Dave Wottle. "Inch by inch means that you set a goal that's off in the distance, and then you keep working toward that goal. I'm very much a management-by-objective-type person. So you set an objective

Olympic gold medalist Dave Wottle crosses the finish line wearing his trademark white hat.

to be the best on your team or the best in the city, state, or nation. Each time you reach one of your objectives, that minor victory becomes motivating. It moves you toward your next objective, which moves you toward your overall goal. It was a lesson that served me well in athletics, as well as in my profession in higher education.

"Because of my tendonitis," Wottle continues, "I was pretty down and disappointed going into the Olympic Games in 1972 in Munich. But Coach Buehler was a tremendous help. I knew that I had to go slowly, and Coach never rushed it. Never. And that kind of steadiness saved my life. You know, any athlete at that level really wants to have his confidence up when he steps onto the track. I can remember Coach Buehler cheering me on in the workouts, giving me encouragement when I ran a pretty good split.

"I was very nervous at the beginning of the 800-meter race. I felt like a wet noodle, like my whole career was coming down to this one moment. In fact, I was so nervous the first 100 meters or so that I fell behind. I was feeling the effects of tendonitis in my left knee, so I didn't know if I could go out fast enough and maintain it. I decided that I wanted to hang back.

"Like any good coach will tell you, you don't catch up all at once. So I was trying to nibble away at the lead. But after the first 400 meters, I was able to regain contact with the back of the pack.

"Then, with about 200 meters to go, I started my all-out kick. I was trying to stay out of trouble on the outside of this race and inch my way up to the lead. Down that home stretch, I was just gaining one inch after another. Then I finally leaned into the tape.

"It was a *very* close race. It took about five minutes for the officials to look at the photo finish—a long time to find out who actually won. Finally, when 'Wottle—USA' flashed up on the screens, it was pretty exciting. I was stunned, in a daze, having won the gold medal by just three-hundredths of a second.

"It took a long time before I could put this experience into perspective. My big takeaway from the Olympic Games is to never give up. The race isn't over until the final step. When you're so far behind in a race like I was, you have thoughts of giving up. You don't think it's going to be possible to win. But you remember what your coach tells you: Just hang in there.

"Inch by inch, that's how Coach took my training. It's a slow and steady pace, sometimes, that wins out in the end."

THINK. ANALYZE. REFLECT.

Inch by inch is not so much about "action" as much as it involves thinking, analysis, and reflection. You have to consider what you do "this inch" to get to "the next inch."

A former student of Coach Buehler's says, "Coach advised us to approach even the simple act of reading a book 'one chapter at a time' so the task wouldn't seem so overwhelming, especially for a student like me with comprehension problems. And the learning strategies he taught got me through my freshman year. In his class, he told us to *write things down* so that we could recall and reflect on what we'd read—and then commit it to memory." As this student found, this thinking not only set the tone for how to approach reading a book, but also for all learning. Reflection is an important ingredient in committing information to memory. And once she developed the patience to follow these steps, as she discovered, her frustration and anxiety were lessened as well.

In an ideal world, this kind of approach to achieving goals, big and small, begins long before we set foot on a track or venture into a boardroom. It starts with helping children learn how to learn: learning how to get organized at home, for example, in order to perform better the next day at school is the foundation of a successful academic career.

It takes a singular focus to learn in this way, according to Susan Ratterree, a special education consultant in New Orleans. "The problem intensifies after third grade," she told *USA Today*, "when harder course work requires children to concentrate. In an age when the diagnoses of such conditions as attention deficit disorder are at an all-time high, learning to focus is even more important."

Once a person—child or adult—sees success using inch-by-inch thinking, it can become a habit. And once it becomes a habit, it is more likely to become an unconscious way of behaving, of staying on task and, eventually, accomplishing dreams.

GOOD TO GREAT

Inch-by-inch thinking underlies many of the ideas of the great thinkers in business. Jim Collins, author of *Good to Great* and *Built to Last*, articulates the stages involved in building a successful organization, including disciplined people (having the "right people on the bus"), disciplined thought ("retaining the unwavering faith that you can and will prevail"), and disciplined action (operating within a framework of responsibilities). While each of these stages echoes Buehler's Coachables, it is Collins's analogy of the flywheel that so vividly relates the inch-by-inch Coachable to the world of business. According to Collins's *Good to Great* concept summary: "In building greatness, there is no single defining action, no grand program, no one killer innovation, no solitary lucky break, no miracle moment. Rather, the process resembles relentlessly pushing a giant, heavy flywheel in one direction, turn upon turn, building momentum until a point of breakthrough, and beyond."

As Coach says, inch-by-inch thinking makes everything a cinch—his athletes and students learned this valuable lesson, and the good people of Durham can testify to it when they hear the church bells ringing on Sunday mornings.

Finish Line Wisdom

THINK. ANALYZE. REFLECT.

Inch-in-inch is not as much about action as it is
about a conscious approach to reaching your goals.
You have to consider what you do "this inch"
to get to "the next inch," when to fine-tune your plan,
and the implications of each decision.

HAVE A PLAN.

Knowing where you are headed
and how you are going to get there
will be the surest guarantee of success.

BREAK DOWN THE TASK AT HAND INTO MANAGEABLE PIECES THAT CAN BE ACCOMPLISHED, LITTLE BY LITTLE.

As you achieve each goal along the way
to your ultimate objective,
you will find motivation and satisfaction at every step.

SEVEN

Persistence. Persistence. Persistence.

Ambition is the path to success. Persistence is the vehicle you arrive in.

—SENATOR BILL BRADLEY, NBA HALL OF FAMER

STARTING LINE WISDOM

There's a reason why Coach doesn't use the word "persistence" only once when he offers this Coachable. Instead, he uses it three times, which reinforces its very definition! Being persistent not only takes resoluteness in the face of opposition but also demands repetition. You don't always reach the goal the first time you try or even the second or third time. You may have to practice for years—or just five minutes. And persistence is the fuel for the soul to do so!

"Sports fill a nifty little spot in our lives," as Coach puts it, "and when it comes to persistence, those who work harder and want it more are the top ten percent of the competitors."

Olympian Joan Benoit (left) and Ellison Goodall (center) compete in the 1979 Miller Lite Invitational at Duke's Wallace Wade Stadium.

Olympian Dave Wottle got this message: "When you have a goal in front of you, you don't want to ever give up. Sometimes you don't make big strides all at once; but the trophy goes to that person who sticks with it, slowly but surely reaches out for that goal, and finally achieves it. That's what I learned from Coach."

Whatever it takes to meet your goals—on and off the field—persistence is the trait that you need to win. It is the engine that pushes you along the way.

PAY YOUR DUES

In light of today's quick-fix, hurry-up, and entitlement thinking, too many people do not see the value of persistence to reach their goals. Coach tells the story of one of his former students who had set his sights on becoming a creative writer for an advertising agency. He had been hired quickly out of school, but his job consisted of writing replies for a client's social media program. He complained to Coach that this wasn't the kind of writing he expected to be doing. He wanted to work on major campaigns. Only two weeks into the job, he was thinking about quitting.

Buehler reminded his former student of this Coachable: With persistence, he explained, it's possible to keep the job, build up your résumé and your reputation for quality work, and be ready to slip into the next opening for a creative writer at this firm or another. In the end, persistence paid off. He stuck with it and worked his way up the company to the job he always dreamed of: creative director. And while Coach doesn't take credit for his former student's success, he is justifiably proud that his student does.

Persistence doesn't mean just being dogged and inflexible in pursuit of a goal. Persistence also means that when you get knocked down, you get up and try again. "If you are playing in this business of athletics, there's always somebody who can clean your clock, so to speak," says Coach. "So when that happens, you go back to work, back to the drawing board. You ask yourself: 'What could I do differently?' When something doesn't go right, there's a reason. Upsets are not meaningless. Sometimes you or your team just didn't make a certain adjustment."

THE HEART OF THE MATTER

Most coaches, Buehler included, will encourage their athletes to watch movies like *Hoosiers* or *Rocky*. While the most immediate message from these stories may be the rewards of persistence, another force is at work: heart. In these movies, the winners aren't necessarily the most talented players, but they are the ones that have an extraordinary passion to achieve the goal. Persistence with heart is an unbeatable combination. The more you care about a goal, the more energy, commitment, and focus you'll employ to reach it, whether it's winning a new job or a track meet.

Coach knew that his role was to be a cheerleader for persistence. When asked about why this Coachable means so much in his life as a teacher, father, and coach, Buehler remarked: "Most of us aren't so vain that we just pat ourselves on the back every day. Sometimes we just flat-out flunk. But we have to go back and fix things. And that takes persistence. We all have moments of doubt. That's what's so important about those in our lives who help us—our parents, teachers, and mentors—and encourage us to keep trying."

What do loving, caring parents do when babies are learning to walk? They cheer them on, applauding their accomplishment, step by step, from sitting up to standing, to crawling, and finally, to navigating the world in an upright position. As every child grows from infancy to adulthood, persistence—and the encouragement that fuels it—will surely lead to not only meeting short-term goals but also the long-term victory.

Winner of the first women's Olympic marathon, Joan Benoit Samuelson modeled persistence throughout her track career, coupling that persistence with tremendous heart as well as the wisdom to make the right decisions for herself.

U.S. runner Joan Benoit of Freeport, Maine, waves the American flag after her gold medal win in the Olympic women's marathon that concluded in the L.A. Memorial Coliseum. August 5, 1984.

"When I first started running," she said, "I was so embarrassed I'd walk when cars passed me. I'd pretend I was looking at the flowers.

"If it hadn't been for all those women who loved the sport of running and who wanted to push themselves as far as they possibly could, I don't know if my success would have been possible or if our sport would be where it is today. It was a strong, persistent sorority of women.

"I was in the right place at the right time, very passionate, and wanted to push myself as hard and as far as I could go."

Mid-career, Samuelson noted: "Every time I fail, I assume I will be a stronger person for it. I keep on running figuratively and literally despite a limp that gets more noticeable with each passing season, because for me there has always been a place to go and a terrible urgency to get there.

"Why I had such a sense of persistence, I can't really tell you," she reflected, concerning that sense of urgency. "I grew up with three brothers and it was survival of the fittest! I just loved to run and had people that shared that same passion and wanted to support my dreams, like Al Buehler."

Finish Line Wisdom

**YOU DON'T ALWAYS REACH THE GOAL
THE FIRST TIME YOU TRY, OR EVEN THE SECOND.**

Persistence is the fuel for the soul to
keep believing that you can win!

**THOSE WHO WORK HARDER, ARE MORE PERSISTENT,
AND "WANT IT" MORE ARE THE TOP TEN PERCENT
OF THE COMPETITORS.**

There's always somebody who can "clean your clock."
When that happens, go back to the drawing board
and ask, "What can I do differently?"

**PERSISTENCE WITH HEART IS AN
UNBEATABLE FORMULA.**

The more you care about a goal, the more energy,
commitment, and focus (heart) you'll employ to reach
it, whether it's winning a new job or a track meet.

BE A CHEERLEADER OF PERSISTENCE.

We all have moments of doubt. That's what's so
important about those in our lives who help us—
our parents, teachers, and mentors—
and encourage us to keep trying.

Be a cheerleader for others—and for yourself.

EIGHT

Il Dolce Far Niente
(The Sweet Art of Idleness)

Rest is not idleness, and to lie sometimes on the grass under trees on a summer's day, listening to the murmur of the water, or watching the clouds float across the sky, is by no means a waste of time.

—SIR JOHN LUBBOCK

STARTING LINE WISDOM

"I believe that part of what makes Coach so calm is that he got to spend some time sailing on his skipjack up in the Chesapeake Bay," Robbie Perkins observed. "This gave him a sense of peace and relaxation. Then he could come back to his work and put all his energy into the track and running the cross-country programs."

Perkins witnessed—and Coach understood—that in order to take care of others you have to first take care of yourself. Coach always knew that "work-life balance" (a phrase commonly bandied about today but not so much a half century ago) is at the heart of a happy, useful life.

Captain Coach Buehler sails the Caribbean. 2004.

The sweet art of idleness is not simply doing nothing, but implies adopting a relaxed attitude even in the most stressful situations that allows you to take a break—whether it is for a few minutes, hours, or days. "Idleness is the same feeling that I have when I crawl into bed at the end of the day," Coach says. "I get rid of all of those aches and pains. I'm finished. I'm relaxed. Without idleness, I'm wound up like a clock! If I didn't make time for idleness, I'd go bananas!"

He may have been a bit facetious in his comment above, but there is much truth to his statement. Research reported in the 2009 issue of *Psychosomatic Medicine* has shown that individuals who spend more time on restorative activities (like spending time in nature, taking vacations, meditation and mindfulness, doing enjoyable activities with their friends, or even spending time on a hobby) not only have greater life satisfaction but they also have lower blood pressure and sleep more soundly at night.

Although controlled research on relaxation is relatively recent, there is considerable evidence documenting its stress-reduction benefits. According to an article in *Brain, Behavior, and Immunity* in August 2008, preliminary research has also shown that practicing mindfulness can lead to improved immune function and a higher quality of life.

The concept that the mind is important in the treatment of illness is integral to the healing approaches of traditional Chinese medicine and Ayurvedic medicine, as well, dating back thousands of years. Hippocrates noted the moral and spiritual aspects of healing, and thought that treatment could occur only with consideration of attitude, environmental influences, and natural remedies.

Coach practices his own brand of idleness by sitting on the front porch, taking walks on the beach, navigating the walking trail near Duke, which bears his name—and sailing. Coach waxes poetically about how his love for the sea began. "My parents exposed me to the sea," he says. "My mom and dad loved to go to the beach, walk along and look for seashells, and talk about the tide. Sitting on the edge of the waterfront and watching the sunset are calming moments in my life. I can watch the sea for hours. There's something about nature, the waves. They're soothing, calm."

While sailing in itself might not *look* like idleness, Coach brought the same "relaxed attitude" to every aspect of his life as he did to his chosen pastime. He observed that when "you are at the mercy of the weather . . . you have to control the boat to do what you want it to do. There are wonderful times and scary times. You take the good with the bad. You can't have everything be exactly perfect. You take the bumps in life along with the good things in life."

While Coach admits that sailing was a big thing for him, in part because he could do it with his family, he sums up the importance of idleness like this: "You see, if you're a busy person, you understand it. You need to be by yourself to be idle. It's a healing process."

IL DOLCE FAR NIENTE

"There is a sign in our houseboat that reads *Il Dolce Far Niente*, which means 'the sweet art of idleness,'" says Buehler's wife, Delaina. "As soon as Al walks through its screen door, he stops worrying about everything. It's the place he goes to get away from it all.

"We all need a place like that. We need to practice the sweet art of idleness every now and then, although we don't want it to overcome our lives. That would be a terrible life, to be idle all the time!

"In track and field and cross-country, you're on a team; but you're really in competition with yourself. Sailing is kind of like that. Al loves sailing and is an excellent sailor. When he has a great sailing day, he'll tell you that he's in harmony with nature.

"We've sailed through some pretty rough seas, and Al has always brought us home safe and sound. I have never doubted that Al Buehler would help us get there.

"That's a pretty good note to end on."

Finish Line Wisdom

**FINDING A PERFECT BALANCE BETWEEN
"WORK" AND "LIFE" IS AT THE HEART
OF A "HAPPY, USEFUL" LIFE.**

Take the opportunity to refresh yourself so that you
can tackle the hard things with energy and passion.

**THE SWEET ART OF IDLENESS IS
NOT JUST ABOUT DOING NOTHING.**

A relaxed yet conscious attitude to everything in
your life allows you a break—
a moment, an hour, a day—
from the stresses that come your way.

EVERYTHING MAY NOT BE PERFECT.

Mindfulness allows you to recognize what you can
control and to let go of what you can't.

Coach Al Buehler's Athletic and Professional Accomplishments

UNIVERSITY OF MARYLAND

Southern Conference Indoor three-quarter mile Champion, 1949

Southern Conference Indoor 880-yard Champion, 1951

Southern Conference Outdoor 880-yard Champion, 1951

Southern Conference Indoor 880-yard Champion, 1952

DUKE UNIVERSITY

Head Men's Cross-Country Coach, 1955–1999

Assistant Men's Track and Field Coach, 1955–1964

Head Men's Track and Field Coach, 1964–2000

Director of Track and Field, 1997–2000

Chair of the Department of Health, Physical Education, and
    Recreation, 1987–2006

Duke Athletics Hall of Fame, 2005

Coach Buehler proudly participates in the Olympic
Torch Relay at Duke University as it makes its way to
the Olympic Games in Atlanta. 1996.

ACCOMPLISHMENTS

Coached 12 NCAA Champions

Coached 10 All-Americans

Coached 7 Penn Relay Champions

Coached 6 ACC Championship Cross-Country Teams

Coached 5 Olympians

Al Buehler Trail, named in his honor

INTERNATIONAL TRACK AND FIELD COACHING

Pan American Games, Head Manager, Cali, Columbia, 1971

Pan Africa–USA International Meet, Meet Director, 1971

MLK Jr. International Freedom Games, Meet Director, 1973

USSR-USA International Meet, Meet Director, 1974

USA–Pan Africa–West Germany Meet, Meet Director, 1975

U.S. Olympic Track and Field Staff/Manager, 1968, 1972, 1984, 1988

Gold Rush Meet, Meet Director, 1996

NCAA Track and Field Championships, Meet Director, 2000

World Indoor Championships, Head Manager for U.S. Contingent, Lisbon, Portugal, 2001

U.S. Jr. National Team, Head Coach, Winnipeg, Canada, 2002

NATIONAL LEADERSHIP POSITIONS AND AWARDS

Former Chairman, NCAA Track and Field Rules Committee

Elected, North Carolina Sports Hall of Fame, 1989

ACCOMPLISHMENTS

Elected, U.S. Track Coaches Association Hall of Fame, 2003

Subject, feature documentary, *Starting at the Finishing Line: The Coach Buehler Story*, 2010

Recipient, Jackie Robinson Humanitarian Award, U.S. Sports Academy, 2011

Acknowledgments

He gives a thousand thanks, and he esteems himself happy
that he hath fallen into the hands of one (as he thinks) the
most brave, valorous, and thrice-worthy . . .
—WILLIAM SHAKESPEARE, *HENRY V*

It all began with a wait list. I walked in Coach Buehler's History and Issues of Sports seminar, hoping to get off the dreaded wait list. Freshmen at Duke are required to take a seminar class, and I soon learned that Coach's class was one of the most popular and atypical.

For starters, it wasn't taught in your ordinary classroom but in his cozy office. The textbooks were ESPN's *SportsCentury* books, and the desks were a combination of benches, chairs, and couches that once belonged to Duke legends like Wallace Wade of Duke's Wallace Wade Stadium. The walls were covered with team trophies, framed photos, and tarnished plaques, a living archive from his forty-five years as head men's track coach.

Hanging in the corner, covered in plastic, was his official jacket from the 1984 Olympics.

I couldn't wait to hear stories from this passionate, energetic man who everyone called "Coach." At the end of the class, I walked up to introduce myself and inquire about the wait list. Coach had extended the class size.

I was in.

It was in Coach's class that I developed a deeper understanding of sports and history—an appreciation for how athletes, coaches, fans, and nations had changed, inspired, and sparked social change. Coach was so modest about his accolades that it wasn't until later, after research and interviews, that I became in awe of his role in civil rights, international relations, and women's sports.

A decade later, when I was a producer for NBC's *Today* show, I called Coach to check in and he shared the news of his upcoming birthday—he was turning eighty years young. I knew right then and there that it was time to peel back the layers of his story. A remarkable life story that has not yet been told. Until now.

Directing and producing the documentary *Starting at the Finish Line: The Coach Buehler Story* was the beginning step of my realizing my dream of telling his story, and was completed in time to celebrate Coach's birthday on 10/10/10. I still have chills thinking about the standing ovation that eighty-year-old Coach and ninety-two-year-old Dr. Walker received as they took the stage and raised their hands together, humbled smiles on their faces, after our film's rough-cut screening at Duke.

Timing is everything. John Duff attended a screening of our film at New York's Tribeca Cinemas. He told me that he had a vision of this book, inspired by Coach's words of wisdom shared in the film. Thank you, John, for believing not only in the power of these Coachables and stories but also in my passion for putting the story on the page while staying true to Coach's authenticity and integrity. You exemplify each of these Coachables with your persistence and positive, inch-by-inch coaching to help us enthusiastically reach the finish line!

Thank you, nifty Coach, for adopting me into your family and being an invaluable mentor, friend, and teacher. And most of all, thank you for taking me off the wait list! Who would have thought that doing so would have led to these adventures together? I am eternally grateful for your wisdom, encouragement, and unconditional support and advice.

Thank you, gracious Delaina, for your willingness to share your memories, experiences, house, car, and storage shed! I love our two a.m. talks about life, love, and romantic comedies. And thank you for letting me bake cookies in your oven and being my official taste-tester, along with Coach. I promise to clean up better next time!

Thank you, wonderful Buehler and Ivy families: Bo, Lynn, and Julia Buehler; and Beth, Hunter, Ruthie, and Will Ivy. You opened up your hearts and your beach house to give me a candid view of your parents and grandparents, Coach and Delaina. Thanks for teaching me how to crack crabs, Buehler-style.

Thank you, Grant Hill, for believing in a five-foot-five Dukie from Kansas! It's been a rewarding journey to collaborate in bringing Coach's story to the screen and these pages. Just like everything you do, your passion and commitment never wavers. The glass is always half full.

Thank you, extraordinary athletes, students, friends, and colleagues of Coach. You took considerable time out of your seriously busy lives to sit down with me and chat about the biggest moments of your lives. You opened up about your dreams achieved, courage rallied, challenges faced, and history written by you and Coach, separately and together. Reminiscing, reconnecting, and reuniting you with Coach and each other were three of the many welcome outcomes from this project.

This book would not have been possible without my mom and dad. I am truly honored to write this book with two of the most amazing people I know. Thank you doesn't cut it. I have the best mom, dad, and brother that a girl could ask for. My heart is full. Final shout-out to our puppy, Lucy, for not eating our manuscript.

As Delaina Buehler always says, "Stay sweet."

Photo Credits

PHOTO CREDITS

23: BUEHLER FAMILY

26: DUKE UNIVERSITY PHOTO

34: ASSOCIATED PRESS

37: ASSOCIATED PRESS

44: J. R. PATTERSON

48: BUEHLER FAMILY

54: BUEHLER FAMILY

60: GLENN GIRTMAN

68: THE HERALD-SUN (DURHAM, NC)

73: ASSOCIATED PRESS

76: BUEHLER FAMILY

84: DUKE UNIVERSITY PHOTO

Endpapers: TIM BAKER Duke's Roger Beardmore (left) receives encouragement from Coach Buehler (far right) before winning the race in a dual meet against University of South Carolina. Fall 1970.

About the Authors

Amy E. Unell is the founder of StoryTales Productions based in Los Angeles. She was an Emmy-nominated producer for NBC's *Today* show. Unell produced and directed the feature documentary, *Starting at the Finish Line: The Coach Buehler Story*, narrated by executive producer Grant Hill. A graduate of Duke University, she was a Media Fellow at Duke's DeWitt Wallace Center for Media and Democracy at the Sanford School of Public Policy, and created and taught an undergraduate production course at Duke. She coproduced and directed *DUKE 91 & 92: Back to Back* for Turner Sports, a film reuniting the Duke NCAA Championship men's basketball team from executive producers Grant Hill and Christian Laettner.

Barbara C. Unell is an author and educator promoting social justice and healthy living for more than thirty years through books, community-based programs, and publications. She is the author or coauthor of a dozen books on family and character education, including *Uncle Dan's Report Card*. Barbara, the founder and editor of several national publications, including *Twins*, has spoken widely on finding cooperative solutions to the challenges of living in health and harmony. Serving as an adjunct professor at the University of Missouri-Kansas City, she specializes in cause-related marketing, public relations, and nonprofit strategic planning. She is the mother of twins, Amy Elizabeth and Justin Alex, and lives with her husband, Bob, and their Westie, Lucy, in Kansas City.

Bob Unell is a former teacher, advertising agency owner, and cofounder, with Barbara, of *Twins* and *Kansas City Parent* magazines. Along with Barbara, he is a partner in the Daniel L. Brenner Family Education Center, providing programs in the area of parenting and character education. Bob creates editorial cartoons for the *Kansas City Star*. His work has appeared annually in *Best Editorial Cartoons of the Year* since 2004.